The SNOW QUEEN

A CHRISTMAS PAGEANT

HANS CHRISTIAN ANDERSEN'S

The
SNOW
QUEEN

A CHRISTMAS PAGEANT

Adapted by
RICHARD KENNEDY

Music by
MARK LAMBERT

Pictures by
EDWARD S. GAZSI

A LAURA GERINGER BOOK
An Imprint of HarperCollinsPublishers

For the E-Poos with love
—R. K.

For Chris with love
—M. L.

To my wife with love
—E. S. G.

Author's Note

The Snow Queen has been staged twice in Newport, Oregon. In the first production we used a hundred children on a gymnasium stage. In the second we used about thirty in a theater with all the advantages. The ages of the children were from four or five (the Sparrows, Butterflies, Bees, etc.) to fourteen or so (Kai and Gerda). We used adults for the parts of Grandma, the Snow Queen, the Lapp Woman, Robber Hag and Reindeer. The music for the show can be played by a full orchestra or a piano solo. The songs are in range for young, untrained voices, and there is dancing for both the serious student of dance and those stumbling along as best they can. All performances sold out. Standing ovations!

Hans Christian Andersen created in the Snow Queen one of those puzzling characters touched with an obscure madness. But whatever the Snow Queen's faults, her story gave our community a delightful Christmas show.

You will understand that only snatches of the music are printed here. Complete musical scores and playbooks are available from SNOW QUEEN, Box 138, Newport, Oregon 97369. Inquiries are welcome.

—Richard Kennedy

Cast in order of appearance:

THE CHIEF IMP: *who sits high up and makes mischief*

THE INVENTOR IMP: *who invents props for mischief*

GRANDMA: *Gerda's grandmother*

GERDA: *a young girl*

KAI: *a young boy*

THE SNOW QUEEN: *a chilly lady who freezes boys*

CHICKENS: *who pull the Snow Queen's sleigh*

THREE FLOWERS: *who are in love with love*

CROW: *Sweetheart's boyfriend*

SWEETHEART: *a lady crow with ambitions*

THE LITTLE MAN: *who marries a princess*

THE PRINCESS

THE ROBBER HAG

THE ROBBER GIRL

A REINDEER: *valiant, and patriotic to boot*

THE LAPP WOMAN: *who might be mistaken for Grandma*

Also: SNOWFLAKES, CHILDREN, SPARROWS, BEES *and* BUTTERFLIES, ROBBERS, IMPS *and* ANGELS, FROZEN BOYS

TIME: *about 100 years ago*

ACT I

SCENE 1

Overture

AT RISE: *It is dark, and some several feet above the stage floor there is illuminated the* CHIEF IMP *on his throne, and come to report to him is a lesser* IMP.

CHIEF: Well, what do you want? Why aren't you down there in the world making mischief? The children are on Christmas holiday. They're all happy down there, sledding in the snow, skating and singing. Get down there and make some trouble. And why aren't you groveling?

IMP: Oh, pardon me, Your Most High and Majestic, Vile, Ugly and Swinish, Altogether Wretched, Foul, and Cruel Chief of All the Imps. . . .

CHIEF: Never mind all the titles. It would take a day to say how nasty I am. Stand up. Tell me your business, and then get down there on that piece of dirt and make some trouble among the children. I can't bear to hear all that laughing and singing.

IMP: That is exactly my intention, Your Highness. Let me introduce myself. . . .

C H I E F : Forget the introductions. You're rotten to the core, I can see that right off. If you had a speck of decency about you, you would never have gotten past the guard. What's that thing you're carrying?

I M P : It's a mirror, Your Highness. It's the reason I'm here intruding on your miserable existence. I'm an inventor, you see, and I've invented this mirror. . . .

C H I E F : You? It was *you* who invented the mirror?! A great invention! Well done, that's a good fellow, keep at it. Vanity, vanity, that's wonderful, all that vanity down on earth. We can always use more mirrors.

I M P : No, no, Your Highness, I didn't invent the mirror, but only this particular mirror. It's different from ordinary mirrors. . . .

C H I E F : Aha, an exploding mirror, is that it? Wonderful idea, send a few million on down with the rest.

I M P : Well, I suppose this one *will* explode, in a way of speaking, but its special quality is that it doesn't reflect quite as it should. This mirror has an evil power. All things, when seen in this mirror, appear to be ugly.

C H I E F : They do, do they? Let me have it. Hmmmmm. Well, it seems to work all right. But what good is it? I'm ugly, you're ugly, everything's ugly. What's the use of it?

I M P : Ah, but there's the trick, Your Majesty. Down there on the earth people think that many things are beautiful.

That's the way they see. However, when I send this mirror into the world, with your approval of course, then all the things they thought to be beautiful will instead appear to be vile and ugly. A lovely landscape will look just like boiled spinach when seen in this mirror, all flowers infested with insects, and the most charming face will seem to be a patch of spots and scabs, and the most friendly smile a sneer of advantage and cynicism.

C H I E F : Huh! Good! That's interesting. Very good. I like it. Anything else?

I M P : Oh, the evil of the mirror goes deep, Your Majesty, the wickedness is yet unexplored, even to the very soul.

C H I E F : All right, all right, not a bad idea. How many can you make? How much help do you need? Labor, cost, production figures, all that, write it up and get back to me.

I M P : But no, Your Highness, we're ready to go, right now! There's the beauty of it—I mean the ugliness of it. This single mirror can work enough evil for the entire world. We won't need more. Here's how it's done. With your permission, I'll throw the mirror down to earth and it will break into millions of pieces. "Caaa . . . rashhhh!" And then those scattering pieces will blow and wander all over the world, and when a sliver of the mirror is caught by a human eye— "Owwwwwww!"—like that, then the person will see the world as it truly is, a foul and ugly place, and all human beings merely toad-riders in a fog of desperation and despair.

CHIEF: Yes, and so it is, and so they are, and so is the whole stupid idea of the world in the first place. If I've said it once, I've said it . . .

IMP: Then at last comes the worst of it. That speck of the mirror in the eye works its way inside, and stabs into the heart—"Aiiiiii!!"—like that. And when that happens, it is the end of all the warmth of love and company of friendship.

CHIEF: That's it, that's it! Excellent! That's the enemy, love and friendship! Hand it here again. We'll give it a try, and if it doesn't work, I'll have you exploded. So. I'll do the honors. Let me see. Where are we now? It looks like it's snowing down there.

IMP: Indeed it is, Your Highness. And that would be Denmark, I think. Those are stork nests on the roofs.

CHIEF: All right, might as well start in Denmark. So up with the mirror and down it goes, and much ugliness to 'em all! (*Throws down the mirror with a great crash.*)

Blackout

SCENE 2

LIGHTS UP: *It is wintertime in Denmark one hundred years ago, in GRANDMA's parlor. Outside it is snowing. There is a sofa, a stuffed chair or two, a central table, and a fire warming in the fireplace. It is a grandmother-type parlor,* *with family pictures on the walls, a bookcase, pillows and lap blankets, a vase of flowers, and a cuckoo clock. One door leads off to the kitchen, and at the back of the parlor is a French window, which opens inward.*

Big flakes of snow blow past the window. Then a gust of wind blows the window open inward with a bang, and as snow blows into the parlor the MUSIC of a whirling dance tune begins, and the dancers, SNOWFLAKES, come blowing into the parlor, and they dance.

DANCE OF THE SNOWFLAKES

Allegretto

There are voices from the kitchen, and children's laughter, and as the dance tune ends the SNOWFLAKES duck out the window, leaving it open. GRANDMA enters the parlor, GERDA and KAI following her.

GRANDMA: Watch the clock, Gerda. If we burn the cookies we shall have to make do with biscuits.

GERDA: Yes, Grandma.

KAI: Or maybe the Snow Queen could bring us some ice-box cookies.

GRANDMA: Believe it or not, Kai, as you wish. It is none of my business.

GERDA: And is the Snow Queen out there now, Grandma, flying through the air?

GRANDMA: Always when it snows, Gerda. Look for yourself. Oh, yes, with her eyes like sparkling ice, and her hair flying about her like a snowstorm. But her breath is like the polar wind, and she can freeze the heart. Now who left the window open? Kai, if you please.

KAI: "Always when it snows." The Snow Queen, the Snow Queen! That's just an old story. There's not *really* a Snow Queen.

GRANDMA: Will you close the window, Kai, if you please? *(She sits at the table.)*

KAI: The Snow Queen, that's for children, like you used to scare Gerda and me with stories about wolves, and bears, and robbers. *(Slams window.)*

GRANDMA: Ohhh, mercy! Oh, Kai! Oh, my snaps and laces! I thought someone had shot off a pistol. Your Christmas holiday will be the death of me.

GERDA: Kai, be careful, go home and slam your own windows.

KAI: And I don't care even if there was a Snow Queen. If she came around here I'd throw her into the fireplace and she'd melt.

GERDA: And does she really fly through the air in a sleigh?

GRANDMA: She does indeed, Gerda, glittering like ice, coasting behind great white chickens as fluffy as clouds, and when she comes to earth she is looking for little boys to carry away with her to her northern kingdom, and there in her grand ice palace she freezes them solid.

KAI: She couldn't get me; and if she landed around here I'd *pluck* those chickens for her.

GERDA: But why does she want to kidnap little boys? Why does she freeze them?

GRANDMA: Well, it isn't so much like a kidnapping, Gerda. It is more like . . . they just run off with her. Yes, there it is, and it's all very sad, but they are all very foolish little boys. They think they are going on a wonderful adventure. Oh, yes, she tells them she loves them and makes promises to give them what they want most, but it is all a lie. And why? Nobody knows why. The Snow Queen is a deep mystery, and what use she might have for foolish, naughty boys, I have no idea whatsoever. Kai, take your finger out of my tea!

GERDA: Oh, won't Christmas ever come, and won't I have a white fox muff this year?

GRANDMA: Nothing easier than to have a white fox muff, of course. We shall bake gold pieces to buy one when the cookies are done.

KAI: I know I'm going to get a new sled for Christmas.

GRANDMA: Do you indeed? How delightful the future is, and so easy to see. Look, on the brim of my cup, a tea leaf. I'll read my fortune. Yes, the king is going to ask me to stuff the royal goose, don't you know, and I shall have a kitchen as large as a ballroom, and an oven big enough to roast a bear in. *(The* CLOCK *calls out, "Cuck-oo cuck-oo.")* Ohhh, the cookies! Oh, my buttons and braces, we forgot the cookies . . . ! *(GRANDMA rushes out.)*

GERDA: Oh, Kai, look, did you see? A white fox just jumped past the window. I saw its tail.

KAI: A new sled for Christmas, Gerda, I just know it. And this year I'm going to sled down Kill-Devil Hill. I really am, Gerda. You can come and watch me.

GERDA: Thank you, but I don't care to see you break your neck. Oh, Kai, it *is* dangerous, you know. Children *do* drown under the ice, and get lost in the woods. There are robbers, too, and it *is* dangerous, Kai.

KAI: Don't be afraid, Gerda, not with me around to save you. I can see it now. Gerda is surrounded by bears and wolves and robbers. But the crowd is cheering! "Hooray, here comes Kai! It's that daredevil Kai on the new sled that he got for Christmas!" And like a flying silver bullet, Kai dives off the top of Kill-Devil Hill to the rescue, his pistols blazing. Blam, blam, blam! He shoots all the wolves and bears and robbers. Blam, blam, blam!

But the crowd only cheers the louder! "It's that daredevil Kai! He's rescued Gerda!" And as we zoom away, the people shout, "It's Kai to the rescue, on that new sled he got for Christmas!"

G E R D A : My hero, I'm sure. But truly, Kai, I do worry about you. There's thin ice at the bottom of Kill-Devil Hill. . . . *(From the kitchen comes the* CRASH *of a broken plate, and* GRANDMA *cries out.)*

G R A N D M A : Oh, Gerda, will you please come help me?

K A I : *(Mimics* GRANDMA.*)* Oh, my snaps and laces! I thought someone had shot off a pistol.

G R A N D M A : Gerda, will you please come at once!

G E R D A : Don't go home, Kai. If the cookies are burned, we'll make some punch anyway.

*(*GERDA *goes off to the kitchen, and* KAI *drinks off* GRANDMA*'s tea, then studies the tea leaves in the bottom of the cup.)*

K A I : Aha, there it is! My fortune in the tea leaves, the soggy future. There, it's my new sled! Fast as the wind, Kai is flying through the air. Yes, some children have disappeared. The Snow Queen kidnapped them. There she is in her sleigh, diving into a cloud. Kai dives after her, his pistols blazing! Blam! Blam, blam, blam, blam!

G E R D A : Kai, come here! Look what we have! Kai!

K A I : Blam, blam, blam, blam! *(*KAI *shoots up the parlor and the window before he exits, and then the* SNOW QUEEN *looks in at the window, and opens it a bit, studying* KAI *as he goes off.)*

Curtain

SCENE 3

AT RISE: The next day, outdoors. Snow covers the ground and drops from the trees as the CHILDREN *bustle about, playing and singing.* KAI *with his old sled, and* GERDA *with her skates, and all sing and dance and throw snowballs.*

CHILDREN'S DANCE

(The CHILDREN *sing la, la, la, la, and clap their hands to the music. The dance ends, and the* CHILDREN *get their gear together, skates and sleds, scarfs and hats and bundled coats.)*

CHILDREN: To the plaza, to the pond! Come on everybody! Who's going down Kill-Devil Hill? Who's not afraid? Come on, Kai. School's out! To the plaza, to the pond, to the river. Holiday, holiday, we're free, we're free! Sleds and snow, let's go, skates and ice, hi-ho! Hooray! Come on, let's go!

BOY: Come on, Kai! I'm sledding down Kill-Devil Hill. I am, I really am, I'm not afraid. Come on, you're not afraid, are you?

KAI: Who's afraid? Who's afraid? *(KAI is sitting on the ground, doing some repair on his sled.)* Go on, I'm coming. This old sled is falling apart again. Go on, I'll catch up, go on.

(*The* BOY *goes off with a shout. Only* GERDA *remains with* KAI. *She has skates over her shoulder and a picnic basket in hand. She stands beside* KAI, *looking into the sky.)* Go on, Gerda, I've just got to fix this old thing.

G E R D A : What a beautiful day. How clear and quiet the sky is. Just that little bunch of clouds above us. They look just like great, white, fluffy . . . chickens.

K A I : Ah, this old sled. Might as well throw it away.

G E R D A : Here, let me sit. We'll have our picnic. Now, let's see. There's cheese and bread, but only one apple. And look, a lovely winter rose that Grandma gave me. Now, you may have the first bite of the apple. Here.

K A I : Thank you, Gerda. Those clouds do look like chickens, don't they? Owwwwwww! Something in my eye. Owww, it hurts!

G E R D A : Kai, what's wrong?

K A I : My eye! . . . Something flashed in the sky. Oh, that hurts! Something in my eye.

G E R D A : Ohhh, Kai. Here, let me look. No, no, I don't see anything. That's right, blink some more.

K A I : Yes, that's better. I must have blinked it out.

G E R D A : Maybe it was a pine needle.

K A I : It felt like a needle. Oh, no, where did you get this apple? This is no apple, this is a school for worms. Look, that's a worm hole. Yuk, yuk, yuk!

GERDA: Let me see it. That isn't a worm hole, Kai, that's just a little spot, just a freckle.

KAI: Freckles are ugly.

GERDA: I have some freckles, Kai.

KAI: All the worse for you. And look at this cheese. Look, it's got green mold on it.

GERDA: Where, Kai? No it doesn't, it's perfectly good.

KAI: It's rotten and ugly, just like my rotten, ugly sled, and it's a rotten, ugly day, and you . . . Aiiiiiii! *(Clutches his heart, and doubles up in pain.)*

GERDA: Kai!

KAI: My heart! Ahhhh, that hurts. . . . Ohhhh. . . .

GERDA: Don't move, Kai! Sit still, I'll run for help!

KAI: No, no—wait. It's going away. There. . . . There, now, that's better. It's gone. Whew, it was like being stabbed. But there, it's all right now.

GERDA: Kai, you'd better go home. Maybe it will come back.

KAI: And maybe *you'll* go away. I told you I was all right. Didn't you hear me tell you I was all right? Stop nagging me.

GERDA: I'm not nagging you, Kai! I'm trying to help you. Are you all right, Kai?

KAI: I'm as well as your buggy rose. *(Snatches it from*

GERDA.) Look at this vegetable. It's a parlor for bugs. Let's stomp 'em into the cellar. There! Stomp, stomp, stomp. Death to all ugly roses.

GERDA: Kai, Kai, don't, don't! *(GERDA begins to cry.)* Oh, the poor rose. Oh, Kai, you've ruined our picnic. What's wrong with you, Kai?

KAI: Oh, now you're going to cry, that's just fine. Maybe it will wash away your ugly freckles. Go on, run to Grandma, put your face in her apron.

Cry baby, baby bawl,

I don't give a darn at all!

GERDA: Oh, no, Kai! What's wrong with you, Kai?

KAI: Go on, go on, go home, go home! Ugly, ugly, ugly! *(GERDA runs off, crying.)* How useless and stupid she is anyway. Useless and stupid, like this old sled. It never was a good sled, and now it's just a piece of junk.

*(The SNOW QUEEN's theme is heard (*COME WITH ME*), and from offstage we hear the clucking of CHICKENS, and as KAI watches in wonder, the SNOW QUEEN arrives in her sleigh pulled by six large, white CHICKENS. She glitters like ice, and wears a crown made of ice, and carries a white fox muff and a silver whip. The sleigh pulls up and stops, the CHICKENS stop clucking, and the SNOW QUEEN steps down.)*

SNOW QUEEN: Ah, there you are, and I could see that you were a handsome young man from a thousand feet in the sky. I saw the flash of your eye. And a clever boy, too. Yes, you are right about that sled. It is just exactly as you say, Kai. That is an old, tired sled, not the sled for a fresh young man like yourself. What you want is a brand-new sled.

K A I : How do you know my name? And I *will* have a new sled, a brand-new sled when Christmas comes.

S N O W   Q U E E N : I expect you shall indeed, Kai, and I know many things. Why, perhaps you shall have a new sled sooner than Christmas if you are as brave and as clever as you look.

K A I : Brave enough, I dare say. I'm going to sled down Kill-Devil Hill. Are those chickens tame? And I can do mental arithmetic, even with fractions.

S N O W   Q U E E N : Ha, ha, ha. That should be clever enough. Then tell me, how many chickens are pulling my sleigh, multiplied by . . . two and a half? *(At the mention of the word "chickens," the* CHICKENS *begin clucking again, and the* SNOW QUEEN *taps their heads with her whip.)* Enough now, enough of that.

K A I : Let me think. Six chickens times two and a half. Carry the denominator, and, ahhh . . . that would be fifteen chickens.

S N O W   Q U E E N : That's very good, Kai. You are a brave and clever boy, just as I thought.

K A I : Those chickens don't bite, do they?

S N O W   Q U E E N : Ohhhh, indeed they bite. They bite into the sky. They drink the mist of clouds and eat the hailstones in thunderstorms. And let me tell you, they have grown so large from flying all around the world. They like to dance to show me that they are not so stupid and clumsy as they look. Would you like to see them dance? They are always trying to impress me. I have promised to tell them one day why the chicken crossed the road.

KAI: Can they really dance?

SNOW QUEEN: It has that resemblance, although just between you and me, I am happy I don't have to dance with them. They think they are going to be swans one day, and I never tell them otherwise. Out of harness now, my dears. Smooth your feathers. There they are. They do both a polka and a minuet, although there isn't much to tell between the two. A touch of the whip gets them started, you know. Dance, my darlings.

THE CHICKEN MINUET

(Mozart: Sonata #4, *with chicken clucks added.*)

SNOW QUEEN: That's enough now, enough. Into harness, again, all of you. (*To* KAI.) You were not expecting too much, I hope. That is as graceful as they get when their feet are on the ground. But when we fly through the air they are as beautiful as great snowflakes. We dive to earth with the sleet, and we go as fast as the wind, which is a lovely thing to do.

KAI: Yes, I know. I've done it on my sled. It makes my eyes water.

SNOW QUEEN: Of course that is true for most people, but my eyes never water.

KAI: But how do you cry, then?

SNOW QUEEN: Ah, there you are, you see. The wind is my friend, it blows inside me, and I never cry. I am the Snow Queen.

KAI: The Snow Queen! Then it's true. I've never seen a real queen.

SNOW QUEEN: Are you afraid, Kai?

KAI: I don't think so. You're very beautiful.

SNOW QUEEN: Thank you, Kai. Come, I shall give you a kiss for your gallantry. There. And the beauty of all things is the beauty of coldness, for in coldness there is no change.

KAI: But all things change. The world goes around, and we all go with it.

SNOW QUEEN: The world does not go around at the North Pole, Kai, and I know of other places where nothing changes. There is a place, Kai, where even people do not change, and love lasts forever.

KAI: But of course people change, and so do their feelings.

SNOW QUEEN: Only if they wish to change, Kai, and I do not wish it. Come with me, Kai, and I will show you the magnificent, never-changing world, castles of ice, and chambers of snow. Come, sit beside me in my sleigh. Oh, come, don't be shy. I will show you wonderful things. Here, take this. *(From the fold of her cloak, she takes a magnifying glass and hands it to KAI.)* Now. Catch a snowflake on your sleeve and look.

K A I : Here's one. I've got it. Oh, that's beautiful! It's like a star, like a frozen flower. And another. How beautiful, and entirely different.

S N O W   Q U E E N : Yes, Kai, all of them are beautiful, and there are enough of them to please your eye forever.

K A I : They're wonderful.

S N O W   Q U E E N : The number of them is without number, and they are all my subjects, and do honor to me.

K A I : But look, they're melting, and now they've all melted, and now they're gone.

S N O W   Q U E E N : That is because they have lost faith, and no longer love me. I let them go, and they are no longer beautiful or significant, as you see. Do you love me, Kai?

K A I : I . . . I don't know.

S N O W   Q U E E N : I love you, Kai. Here, give me the glass now, and come for a sleigh ride with me. And I shall tell you all my secrets.

K A I : Secrets? Do you have secrets?

S N O W   Q U E E N : All queens have secrets, Kai. And you may sit close to me, and listen. Come, we'll fly away into the crystal sky.

KAI: But I just can't go off like that. I'll have to go home first. No, first of all I'll run and tell Gerda.

SNOW QUEEN: Forget about Gerda, Kai. She is no use to us, and could never allow us our adventure together, nor could she love you as I love you. And if you come with me, I shall give you a new sled.

KAI: Even before Christmas?

SNOW QUEEN: Ha, ha. Even before Christmas. Oh, how beautiful it will be, Kai. We'll fly through the air and play in the clouds. Oh, how beautiful, the snowflakes and ice. Come with me, Kai. *(She sings.)*

COME WITH ME

Come with me, snowflakes and ice,
Fly to my kingdom, bundled up tight.

Come with me, snowflakes and ice,
Sledding and skating, winter delight.

KAI: I like your singing, and I like you to kiss me.

SNOW QUEEN: Ha, ha. There, now, that is the last kiss you shall get from me, or I should kiss you to death. Brave Kai, clever Kai, take up your sled and mount into my sleigh. Come now, and we shall fly away together on a wonderful adventure. Of course you are not afraid? Of course not. So up you go. There, are we ready? Come into my robe. And now, hold fast there and hold fast to me. Here we go now, for a sleigh ride that will satisfy anyone who can be satisfied.

Away to the sky,
My chickenflakes, fly!

(Off they go, with a great clucking of the CHICKENS.*)*

Curtain

(During the scene change, several SPARROWS *come upon the apron of the stage, and they dance. It is a change of season, from winter to spring.)*

DANCE OF THE SPARROWS

Blackout

SCENE 4

AT RISE: MUSIC. *Outdoors, it is springtime. Blossoming bushes, the trees with leaves, the sun is shining and birds are chirping, bees are buzzing and butterflies are flitting and flirting. Three* FLOWERS *dance and sing.*

A YOUNG MAN'S FANCY

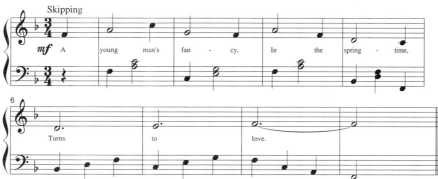

<table>
<tr><td>

A young man's fancy,
In the springtime,
Turns to love.

How nice to know,
A young man's fancy,
Turns to love.

</td><td>

A young man's fancy,
In the springtime,
Turns to love.

It's lovely how,
A young man's fancy,
Turns to love.

</td></tr>
</table>

(As the SONG *ends, the* FLOWERS *and all hear* GERDA *approaching. They hush each other, and the* FLOWERS *stand motionless as* GERDA *comes onstage.)*

GERDA: Hello? Who's there? Is someone about? Hello? I thought I heard singing. No? All alone. Just this lovely meadow. And what beautiful flowers. How Kai would have loved them. How he loved the springtime. Oh, poor Kai, poor Kai, poor Kai.

1ST FLOWER: You oughtn't to repeat yourself like that. It diminishes your authority. You should say, "Poor Kai," just once, and then let the matter drop. Repetition is wearisome and makes a thing sound trivial. I am tired of poor Kai already. But why do you call him poor?

GERDA: Alas, because he is dead. Alas, alas, alas.

1ST FLOWER: Tut, tut, tut-tut-tut-tut-tut-tut. Will you stop repeating yourself. It is bad enough to be dead without all that repetition.

GERDA: Oh, but I loved him, and he is dead. Dead and gone, all since last winter.

2ND FLOWER: That is clearly impossible.

3RD FLOWER: Entirely out of the question.

GERDA: Oh, but he is. Poor Kai.

1ST FLOWER: "Poor Kai!" Is that all you have to say for yourself? Besides, Kai is not dead. We flowers come from under the ground where the dead people are, and Kai is not among them.

GERDA: But everyone says he is dead, and no one has seen him since last Christmas holidays.

2ND FLOWER: There you are. It is clearly a case of mistaken identity. Most likely he is lost in the woods. Not dead, at any rate.

3RD FLOWER: You may forget about it entirely. Off you go, now, and don't pick the flowers.

GERDA: But he has been gone for so long. Everybody says he fell into the river with his sled.

1ST FLOWER: Well, that is a sad story, and very wet, but it isn't true. And you are not the only one with a sad story. Boom-da-boom! Boom-da-boom!

GERDA: Boom-da-boom? What does that mean?

1ST FLOWER: Do you hear the drum? Boom-da-boom. Three notes, always same. A man has died. The Hindu woman in her red garment lies on the funeral pyre with her dead husband. The flames go up all around the dead man and his wife. But the woman is only thinking of the living man who stands in the circle round, whose eyes burn more fiercely than the flames that burn the bodies. And a question rises with the black smoke. "Do the flames of the heart die in the fire?" (*The* FLOWERS *sing and dance.*)

INDIA SONG

I want to know,
Can't comprehend.
Can it be so,
Love never ends.

1 ST FLOWER: Well, what do you think? Were you listening? It would only be polite, you know, to pay attention when you're being entertained, and then to give an opinion when you're asked.

GERDA: I beg your pardon, but I didn't know I was being entertained, and I didn't quite understand what was being asked.

1 ST FLOWER: Didn't understand!

2 ND FLOWER: A mere child.

3 RD FLOWER: She'll want it repeated, I fancy.

GERDA: The song I could understand. It's the story that was difficult.

1 ST FLOWER: Difficult? I should say so! Not that I suppose it matters to you, but one day we flowers will wilt and die, and then we'll be raked up and thrown onto a bonfire. There! Difficult indeed! But the question is—does our love die with us or not?

GERDA: I'm sure I don't know the answer to that.

2 ND FLOWER: Well, you do see the problem, don't you? Only roses live forever.

3 RD FLOWER: At least that's their story.

1 ST FLOWER: But we don't believe everything we hear. Besides, roses are repeatedly falling in love, which diminishes their authority.

GERDA: All I know is that love seems to be quite sad sometimes.

1ST FLOWER: When you are older and have all your petals it will be sadder still, believe me.

3RD FLOWER: The trouble is, she doesn't yet know the true joys of love. Listen carefully, then. There was a man and a maid. She wore a green gown and he all in midnight blue. They danced hand in hand by the edge of a lake in the moonlight, and then he vanished into the forest. She ran after him, searching the darkness. Now a boat like a coffin glides out of the wood toward the lake. A woman lies in the bottom of it, perfectly still. Is she dead? Is she sleeping? Is she quietly thinking things over? (FLOWERS *sing and dance.*)

MY POOR HEART

My love has mortified my,
And brutalized my,
And terrified my
Poor heart.
My love has agonized my
Poor heart
And what am I to do?
Petrified

And crystallized,
And pulverized,
And liquified,
And oxidized,
And vaporized,
And if this is love,
  it should happen to you.

3RD FLOWER: You see, even love does have its lighter, carefree moments.

GERDA: Your song makes me wonder if I want to be in love when I grow up.

1ST FLOWER: Don't miss it, that's my advice, although love does have a way of changing roundabout, and quickly sometimes. Enough to jerk your roots out!

2ND FLOWER: Love is like the wind, you must bend with it.

3RD FLOWER: Love is like the weather, you must be brave with it.

2ND FLOWER: For what would we do without love?

1ST FLOWER: How truly that is said. Love is the warmest and most enriching of all experiences, worth whole loads of fertilizer.

2ND FLOWER: And you are well off, for Kai is not dead. Take courage, you will find him.

3RD FLOWER: Don't trouble yourself about it any longer, or we shall think you are stupid. On your way, now, and be happy with the summer.

GERDA: But it was just springtime.

3RD FLOWER: That was a long time ago.

1ST FLOWER: As for us, we keep up our spirits by singing and dancing.

2ND FLOWER: For life is not so bad.

3RD FLOWER: And we are, after all, quite beautiful.

1ST FLOWER: And the bees come to visit us with the very best of intentions. *(MUSIC.)*

MEDLEY OF THE FLOWERS' SONGS

*(*FLOWERS, BEES, BUTTERFLIES *and all sing and dance, then go off, leaving* GERDA *alone.)*

Blackout

LIGHTS UP: *Some time later. A garden. A pathway winding between nicely cropped bushes, a birdbath, a piece of statuary, a garden chair or two, and in the background, far off, a castle. There is a commotion offstage, and on comes a male CROW followed by his SWEETHEART, who is bopping him with a black muff in one hand, and a book in the other.*

CROW: Ow! Ow! Sweetheart! Ow! Ow! Ow!

SWEETHEART: Ow, ow, ow, indeed! You should get more than that, imbecile! You backward, stupid, blackbird. You, you, bumbling . . . Crow! How ever will I apologize to the Countess?

CROW: What did I say wrong to her? What did I say wrong?

SWEETHEART: Oh, how absolutely *gauche*! Oh, you pitiful fool!

CROW: Pity, that's it, that's what I said. She was telling us about her operation. . . .

SWEETHEART: Oh, the poor woman, a terrible operation, under the knife like that. Thank goodness she was speaking French, I don't think I could have taken it in English.

CROW: Yes, in French. And I said, "What a pity"—"*Quel*

fromage," that's what I said. That's all. *"Quel fromage"* — "What a pity."

SWEETHEART: That does not mean "What a pity." *"Quel dommage"* is "What a pity." *Dommage* is the word, not *fromage*!

CROW: Well, what did I say?

SWEETHEART: You said, "What a cheese." Oh, poor idiot. I will think of something to excuse you, but they will never let you live in the castle with me unless you learn to speak proper French. And now it is time for your lesson. *(Opens book.)* By the way, have you learned to be housebroken yet? That's the very first thing they'll notice.

CROW: I'm working on it, Sweetheart.

SWEETHEART: Good. That's something you'll always find useful. Now. Today we will translate proverbs and epigrams. Along with that, we shall have your dancing lesson. *Attention! Position première! (But just as CROW takes this ballet stance, GERDA comes onstage, and CROW addresses her, attempting an elegant bow.)*

CROW: *Ah. Bonsoir, mademoiselle.*

SWEETHEART: *(Now also sees GERDA, and corrects the CROW's posture.) Le pied gauche, le pied gauche! Comme ça! Comme ça! (Then haughtily to GERDA.)* And who might you be?

GERDA: My name is Gerda, and I've been wandering ever so far. . . .

SWEETHEART: You do curtsy, do you not?

GERDA: Oh, why yes, of course. *(Curtsies.)*

SWEETHEART: *(A sweeping bow.) Enchantée. Parlez-vous français?*

GERDA: I beg your pardon?

SWEETHEART: You do not speak French? What a pity.

CROW: *Quel fromage!*

SWEETHEART: Exactly. And what brings you into our presence, my dear?

GERDA: My friend is lost, little Kai. He has bright blue eyes and is about this tall. . . .

CROW: Ah, the little man, the little man, the mysterious little man!

SWEETHEART: Silence! How many times must I tell you! You must never act surprised about anything. You will be thought quite simple and devoid of experience.

GERDA: A little man? What little man? Have you seen Kai? Then he is alive!

SWEETHEART: There is a little man, and a stranger besides. *Oui*, an interesting story about that one. Most peculiar. However, we are about to begin our lessons. *(Again she opens the book.) Position première.*

GERDA: A story? About a little man? Oh, tell me, tell me, please.

SWEETHEART: Patience, my dear, you must have patience. It is always admired . . . even when you have lost your morals. *(SWEETHEART also assumes the first position. MUSIC.)*

THE FRENCH LESSON

(This is a combination French and ballet lesson. SWEETHEART leads CROW in dancing, and during vamps in the music she reads epigrams in French from the book, and bops CROW with her muff for his errors in translation. As to the dance, it is a sort of ballet burlesque, at least on the part of CROW.)

SWEETHEART: *Sauter de la poêle sur la braise.* Translate.

CROW: Out of the frying pan, and into the choir.

SWEETHEART: *(Bop! Bop!)* Dunce! Imbecile! Dance! (*MUSIC and dance*) *Quand le chat n'est pas là, les souris dansent.* Translate.

CROW: When the cat is away, the mice will sashay.

SWEETHEART: *(Bop!)* Moron! *(Bop!)* Fool! Oh, dance, imbecile. *(MUSIC and dance.)* *Un tiens vaut mieux que deux tu l'auras.* Translate.

CROW: A bird in the hand is worth two in the . . . tush?

SWEETHEART: Oh, nincompoop! *(Bop, bop!)* I am crazy with you! *(Bop, bop!)* *Très* fool! *(MUSIC, to the end of dance.)*

GERDA: Bravo, bravo! *(Clapping.)*

SWEETHEART: *Merci, merci.* Well, not entirely without breeding, I see. Your name was Gerda, did you say?

GERDA: Gerda, yes, and I am looking for my friend. His name is Kai, and he is not dead after all.

SWEETHEART: Indeed, how nice for him.

CROW: That could be the stranger, Sweetheart. He is a little man, and a mystery besides.

SWEETHEART: To those without opinions, *everything* is a mystery. I happen to have very good opinions. Now, then. A while back a little man came to this kingdom. He was poorly dressed, and he had a pack on his back.

GERDA: No, no . . . that would have been his sled.

SWEETHEART: Perhaps, that might be so. I didn't take too much notice. At any rate, he managed to get into the castle on some pretense, and somehow managed to talk with the princess. Well—and who would have believed it—he spoke so cleverly that the princess was all at once charmed with him.

GERDA: Oh, it *was* Kai! He is so clever. When we grow up we're going to be married. He can do mental arithmetic, even with fractions.

SWEETHEART: Really? How droll. Well, you can forget about marrying him. Before there was time even to gossip about it, the princess decided to marry him. And so Kai is a prince now, and he is too majestic to care for you anymore. That is my opinion.

GERDA: Oh, but I must see him. Then I will know he is alive. I must get into the castle.

SWEETHEART: Well, that is very easy to talk about. But how can it be done? Why, you don't know even a word of French.

GERDA: Oh, there must be a way to see him, there must be.

SWEETHEART: Hmmmmmm. *C'est possible, oui.* Sometimes, late in the evening, after the little man—I mean to say, the prince—after he has taken supper and his brandy. . . .

GERDA: Brandy? But Kai never drank brandy, or even wine. Sometimes he might sip some tea. . . .

SWEETHEART: Well, he has taken to strong drink then, and it is all downhill after that. You are lucky to be without him, *n'est-ce-pas?* So . . . it is late evening now. *(LIGHTS down.)* And perhaps he will come to stroll in the garden with the princess.

GERDA: But it was just midday.

SWEETHEART: That was a long time ago. Come, we shall hide behind this bush and wait. You, goose, come behind with us here. Look, we are hidden just in time. Here comes the little man with the princess. Shhhhhhhhh, quiet now. *(To the* CROW.) Attend, you dunce, and learn how to speak cleverly. *Regardez*, listen.

(The LITTLE MAN *strolls across the stage with the beautiful* PRINCESS. *He is a little man, but very old; with a white beard and a cane. The* PRINCESS *is taking notes of his wisdom in a small notebook. The following conversation takes place as they stroll across the stage and off.)*

LITTLE MAN: Oh, yes, my dear, and those are absolute facts I tell you. Yes, yes, well-documented facts. Not worth noting the opinions of the younger set—those young men of the court, half-baked upstarts. . . . But am I speaking too fast?

PRINCESS: *(Writing.)* Young men. Upstarts. I have it.

LITTLE MAN: Yes, yes, yes, though otherwise they might be from the best families. Indeed, they may be upstanding young men, but their ambitious thrusts into areas of which they have the most scant knowledge. . . . But I'm rushing you.

PRINCESS: *(Writing.)* No, no, I have it. Upstanding young men. Ambitious thrusts.

LITTLE MAN: Yes, my dear. The fault being only in their youth, you see. At that age, wisdom and clear judgment is often defeated by the glands. Yes, yes, yes. And, alack the youth of it all, they are overtaken by these adolescent bursts of energy.

PRINCESS: *(Writing.)* A moment. A moment, sir. Upstanding young men. Unruly glands. Adolescent bursts of energy. There.

LITTLE MAN: Ahem. Yes, well. Scratch that out. Let me put it another way. You see, my dear, only a mature man, who has lived a long life can really appreciate, ah . . . how to say it? *(They continue strolling, the speech trailing and fading as the* LITTLE MAN *and the* PRINCESS *go off.)* An analogy with wine might serve. As we all know, that wine which is aged by the years, not of a short season, but has the advantage of a long, long, long, aged and long, time and the age of a long, old and long, long and old and aged. . . .

GERDA: Oh, that wasn't Kai at all. Why didn't you say he was such an old man?

SWEETHEART: My dear, one is hardly surprised

about anything these days, is one? And what could be more *outré* than to mention the difference in your ages.

C R O W : Sweetheart is right, of course, she's quite a bit older than myself, but I never ... *(SWEETHEART bops him good.)*

G E R D A : Oh, dear, now what shall I do? Where shall I go?

S W E E T H E A R T : I should search to the north if I were you. I mean to say, if you were carrying a sled, which way would you go, my dear? And I hear that the northern fashions are divine this autumn.

G E R D A : Autumn? But it was just summer. I was talking with the flowers.

S W E E T H E A R T : That was a long time ago. *(To CROW.)* Do you hear? —talking to flowers, if you can imagine it.

C R O W : Follow the North Star. There's the Big Dipper, and it points the way. You'll have to go through the woods. There are robbers, so take care. They'd kill you for your petticoat. It will be dreadfully cold, and you're hardly dressed for it. Sweetheart, a gift of your muff, perhaps? *Un geste?*

S W E E T H E A R T : *(Bops him.) Bien sûr!* Here you are, my dear.

G E R D A : Oh, thank you very much.

S W E E T H E A R T : *Noblesse oblige.*

CROW: Take care. It is said that the robbers eat children.

SWEETHEART: And if you meet any civilized people, I suggest that you learn enough French at least to read a menu. *(CROW and SWEETHEART begin moving off.)*

GERDA: Good-bye. Thank you very much, thank you. Good-bye.

SWEETHEART: *Il n'y a pas de quoi. Au revoir.*

CROW: If you get frightened by the dark, whistle a brave tune. *Bonne chance!* I wish you luck. *Adieu, adieu!*

GERDA: I do, too. Good-bye, good-bye.

(CROW and SWEETHEART depart, CROW whistling the Marseillaise as best he can, as SWEETHEART bops him with the book.)

SWEETHEART: Get on pitch, you tin-eared moron. The key of G, and count the measure, you idiot. Do you call that patriotic? They would hang you for treason. Can't you learn a thing right? *Mon Dieu. Mon Dieu!* You utter dunce, I am exasperated on you! *(Bop, bop, and off.)*

GERDA: The North Star. Now there's the Big Dipper, and the cup points to the North Star, and so my direction is . . . Oh, no, now I must go directly into the woods. Well, I shall think of Kai. He would do the same for me. And surely, ha, ha, robbers do not eat little girls.

And I'll whistle. Now how did that lovely dance tune go? Oh, yes.

(*And* GERDA *begins walking offstage bravely, whistling the* FRENCH LESSON *tune. She is gone for a few moments when the* ROBBER HAG *and her* ROBBER BAND *come onstage, sniffing the air and stooping to study tracks.* ROBBER MUSIC *up.*)

H A G : (*Sniff, snuff!*)   It's something to eat, no doubt about it. (*Sniff, sniff.*) Walking on two legs. By St. Nose, we're on the track. Something tasty passed this way, and it's wrapped in clean linen. (*Sniff, snuffle.*) Ha, ha, it's a little girl. That's the smell of it. She'll do for the pot. Not dressed in rags, either. Ha, ha, tonight we'll dine on our betters. We're on the track. Off that way, to the north. Roast child, yum, yum!

C u r t a i n

E N D   A C T   O N E

Overture

LIGHTS UP: *The* "INVENTOR" IMP, *leading a goose, grovels up to the* CHIEF IMP *on the apron of the stage.*

CHIEF: Well, who are you and what's your business? And stop groveling. Grovelers are always up to something. What are you up to?

IMP: Your Highness, I was here before. I'm an inventor. I invented a mirror. . . . Surely Your Highness remembers. You held the mirror in your own hands. You looked very ugly in it.

CHIEF: That's right, that's right, now I remember. Quite repulsive, if I do say so myself. You can't fool a mirror. Well done, that was a good idea. So—what do you have now? What's the goose for?

IMP: It's my latest invention, Your Highness. It's a wild goose. They're impossible to chase down, you know. Maybe you've heard about that.

CHIEF: Impossible, yes, but where did you get that one?

IMP: I ordered it out of a catalog, Your Highness. But you see, if we let about a million of them loose in the world. . . .

CHIEF: Good, good, I got it. A wild-goose chase, an absolute waste of time for everybody. Fine, breed 'em up and let 'em loose. But how's the mirror project going? Everything ugly down there?

IMP: There are prospects, Your Highness. Most recently, I can report to you about a boy and a girl who are in love. . . .

CHIEF: Yaaaaaaa! *Never* say that word to me! I can't *stand* that word! I'll have you shot at dawn if you ever say that word again!

IMP: Your Highness. How shall I put it, then? A sort of, ah, boy-girl "thing" is happening. Her name is Gerda, and his name . . .

CHIEF: Never mind the names. Names are unimportant. And so, he (that word) her, and she (that word again) him. Is that how it is?

IMP: Yes, Your Highness. It's a classic . . . (that word) story. Of course we'll fight it. Some special-force Imps are going down. A battle might be expected, and because (that word) is in danger, Angels will come to fight on their side.

CHIEF: Yaaaaaaaaa! If you ever mention "Angels" to me again I'll have you molested by alligators! At dawn. You may call them "religious flying objects," and I'll quite understand.

I M P : Your Highness.

C H I E F : All right, all right, then. Let's see what we've got here. A battle coming up with those miserable "flying objects." Good, remember to fight dirty. That's an order, pass it around.

I M P : Yes, Your Highness, and I should mention that the Snow Queen is part of the story.

C H I E F : What? The Snow Queen? Are you certain of that? Well, whatever else, we fight on the side of the Snow Queen. There's no question about that.

I M P : Yes, Your Highness, we always have.

C H I E F : And always will, so long as I'm the Chief. Do you have a problem with that?

I M P : Your Highness.

C H I E F : Did . . . ah, did you see the Snow Queen? How did she look? Did you talk with her?

I M P : Your Highness, only a passing comment or two, about the weather. . . .

C H I E F : Uh-huh, well, what's the story down there now? Is the Snow Queen on?

I M P : We can watch, Your Highness. So far, the story goes like this: The Snow Queen has stolen Kai away and flown to her kingdom with him.

C H I E F : Kai? Who's Kai?

I M P : He's a boy, Your Highness. The Snow Queen took a fancy to him.

C H I E F : She did, did she? Kidnapping. That's bad.

I M P : But now—there, you see, the scene is deep in the forest. The robbers have caught Gerda and will probably eat her.

C H I E F : Did she . . . ah . . . did she say anything about me?

I M P : Who? Gerda, Your Highness?

C H I E F : Gerda? Who's Gerda?

Blackout

SCENE 2

A T   R I S E : *Nighttime, deep in the forest. The* ROBBERS' ENCAMPMENT. *There is a small campfire, a large pot, some equipment about, and sleeping pads. The* HAG *and* ROBBERS *come trooping onstage.* GERDA *is pushed along with them, bound with a rope. A little* ROBBER GIRL *enters last, pistol and dagger in her belt, leading her* REINDEER.

H A G : *(Dagger in hand, poking* GERDA.) Ha! Don't you worry, this old nose can still smell a sweet, plump little girl. She is fat and pretty, eh? She is as good as a fat little lamb, and how nice she will taste. More logs on the fire, there, get it boiling, and we'll strip the little beggar for the pot.

ROBBER GIRL: *(Drawing her knife.)* No, you won't, old mother boney bones! You shan't eat her! I'll eat *you* first! I'll stuff *you* into the pot!

(The ROBBER GIRL jumps on the ROBBER HAG's back and bites her, and when she is thrown off the two tussle on the ground, a good yelling battle, and then the ROBBER GIRL stands free, protecting GERDA.)

HAG: Ow! Ow! You wild, wicked child, you'd bite your own mother, you horrid, wayward little beast.

ROBBER GIRL: You shan't hurt her. She shall play with me and sleep with me. I'll cut your beard off if you hurt her.

HAG: Spoiled brat! I'll cut some more holes in your ears! Hey, hey, they can hang you from your ears.

ROBBER GIRL: Hang you from your nose, old mother snot!

(Both with knives flashing, the HAG goes for the ROBBER GIRL, who latches on to her arm, biting, and they go yelling around and tumble onto the ground, while the ROBBERS urge them on as before.)

ROBBERS: Ho! Now we'll have some blood. Look at the old bear dancing with her cub. We'll skin the loser. They'll eat each other up. Bite her, scratch her, stick her, kick her! *(Etc.)*

HAG: *(Parting from the tussle.)* Ow! Ow! Ohhh, all the grief a loving mother has. Oh, ungrateful child. Serpent's tooth! Better I should have drowned you in mother's milk! You were a brute of a baby! Where's my bottle? I'll teach you after I drink from my bottle, see if I don't. Where's my rum, where's my bottle?

ROBBER GIRL: Go find your bottle and fall into your bottle. When you're good and pickled, we'll eat *you*.

(*The* ROBBER GIRL *cuts* GERDA's *bonds and sits protectingly next to her. The* HAG *finds her bottle and sits drinking resentfully. The other* ROBBERS *tighten gear, talk slobber among themselves and do camp chores, and one by one retire to their sleeping pads during the following.*)

GERDA: Oh, thank you, thank you, I've been awfully afraid. I was warned about robbers.

ROBBER GIRL: Don't thank anyone too soon for a favor. It may be a trick.

GERDA: But you must be a friend. They would have killed me.

ROBBER GIRL: And I may kill you yet. But don't worry, they shan't kill you as long as I don't get cross with you. So they all get to go to bed hungry. I like that. I like to send my mother to bed without her supper.

GERDA: But surely, they wouldn't have eaten me.

ROBBER GIRL: They *would* have eaten you, and spit out your name for the dogs. What is your name?

GERDA: My name is Gerda, and I'm searching . . .

ROBBER GIRL: That's a lovely black muff you have. Give it here. Now it's mine. Are you a princess?

GERDA: Oh, no, not a princess at all, and I haven't any gold for you to rob. I am only searching for my friend, Kai, who has been lost since last winter.

ROBBER GIRL: That may be so, but I don't believe everything I hear. *(To the* REINDEER.*)* Lapland! You, yes, you, wet nose—come closer here. Give me your reins. He breathes on me when I sleep to keep me warm, but tonight you shall sleep with me and keep me warm. Would you like to see him dance? I tickle his throat with my knife like this, and doesn't it frighten him? Ha, ha. Look at him jump. Ha, ha, ha. He is so comical. But those are the only steps he knows. Now, kiss him. It makes him feel human and gives him hope.

GERDA: Oh, no, must I? Oh, no!

ROBBER GIRL: Kiss him, or I shall tickle *you!*

GERDA: *(Kisses the* REINDEER.*)* Ugh! Am I a prisoner now?

ROBBER GIRL: You're a *robber* now. I'll teach you everything I know. If you learn fast you won't get caught and hanged, and it's wonderful fun if you don't get hanged. But now it's time to sleep. Come, this is my pad. Come, down here, down here with me.

GERDA: Do you always sleep with a knife in your hand?

ROBBER GIRL: Of course I do. You never know what may happen. That's your first lesson. Now be quiet and sleep. *(In a few moments, the* ROBBER GIRL *begins snoring, and the* REINDEER *moves closer and whispers to* GERDA.)*

R E I N D E E R : I believe your story. The wood pigeons were talking, and I heard them. Your friend Kai was in the Snow Queen's sleigh, flying through the air behind six white chickens. They were low over the trees where the wood pigeons were in their nest. The Snow Queen blew her breath on the young ones and all died save two. She was taking Kai far away to her northern kingdom.

G E R D A : Oh, Kai, oh, Kai! Grandma told us, and now she'll freeze him forever. Oh, Kai, oh, Kai!

R O B B E R   G I R L : All right, now, I'm trying to sleep! That's enough gossip. That hairball will talk you to death if you let him. Now lie still, or you'll get this knife in your tummy.

G E R D A : Ohhhhhhhhhh. Ohhhhhhhh.

(LIGHTS *down slowly, and up slowly. It is morning.* GERDA, *the* ROBBER GIRL, *and the* REINDEER *are at the camp alone, sitting at the fire and drinking out of cups.)*

R O B B E R   G I R L : So then . . . I'd rather be out robbing, but today it's my turn to guard the camp. The Snow Queen, eh? Oh, yes, I've heard of her. She's a robber, too, in her own way. But what use she could have for frozen boys, I wouldn't know. They're not much good even when they're warm. And she travels behind six white chickens. That's a nice trick, having your supper pull your sleigh. The Snow

Queen, yes, glittering and beautiful, so they say, and she carries a silver whip and a big white fox muff. Now there's a prize. I'd like to get my hands on that white fox muff.

GERDA: Then it could be true, what the wood pigeons said? Kai was stolen away by the Snow Queen?

ROBBER GIRL: Yes, yes, probably so. Wood pigeons don't lie. They haven't the imagination for it. Well, since Kai is only a boy there's not much loss there. It's much more fun to go with robbers, you'll see.

GERDA: Oh, but I must find him! The Snow Queen might have started to freeze him already. Kill me to stop me, but I've got to go to him. But, but . . . which way should I go?

ROBBER GIRL: "Which way should I go?" Listen to her. Sit down, sit down before you get lost. Ha, ha, so there it is. You love this Kai, is that it?

GERDA: Oh, yes, for as long as I can remember.

ROBBER GIRL: You'd better love him. The Snow Queen lives almost at the North Pole, and there's dangers all the way—wolves, and bears, and whatnot.

GERDA: Whatnot?

ROBBER GIRL: That's the worst of it, and so forth. Oh, yes, you'd better love him. The journey will probably kill you.

GERDA: Well, but I am going to him. Let me see, which way is north?

ROBBER GIRL: Listen to her, our apprentice hero—"Which way is north?" Sit down, sit down again and warm yourself while you have the chance. That's a long, cold journey. And first you must go to the Lapp Woman's hut. That's on the way. She might help you unless, of course, she doesn't. She fools around with visions, and prophecy, and all that sort of nonsense. Yes, you'll have to visit the Lapp Woman first. That's way up in Lapland. *(At this mention, the* REINDEER *stands at attention, and salutes always as he sings this* SONG.*)*

ANTHEM

Oh, Lapland, sweet Lapland,

We raise our antlers high,

Oh, Lap, Lap, Lap, Lap, Lap, Lap . . . (Etc.)

ROBBER GIRL: As you were, stew meat! At ease and shut up! That's right. That's where I caught this beast. Lapland. That's their national anthem, for reindeer anyway.

REINDEER:

Oh, Lapland, sweet Lapland,

We raise our antlers high,

Oh, Lap, Lap, Lap, Lap, Lap, Lap . . . (Etc.)

ROBBER GIRL: Shut up again! All that patriotic blubbering gives me the fantods. But never mind. If you're going, you're going. But you'd never get there on your own.

Here's a pack for the journey. *(To the* REINDEER.*)* Get into it, fuzz-face. There's food in here and other things you'll need. And you, big ears, see you lead my little playmate to the Lapp Woman's hut. And bring her back safely or I'll have your liver for supper when I catch you again.

GERDA: Oh, thank you, thank you, dear friend, very, very much.

ROBBER GIRL: Don't whimper. Robbers shouldn't whimper, and you're going to be some excellent robber if you can get Kai away from the Snow Queen. It's dreadfully cold where you're going, but I'll keep your muff. It's much too pretty. But you can take this scarf. It's my mother's. And take these gloves of hers. I'll say you stole them, and she'll be satisfied. She'll believe anything after she's been at her bottle. It's then she likes to stroke my hair and kiss me. *(ROBBER GIRL sniffs and wipes her nose on her sleeve.)* What nonsense. And what else? Give me those pretty shoes and take my fur boots. And here's my warm hat for you. Oh, if they catch you wearing my hat and my boots they'll hang you for sure. Ha, ha, ha. Off you go, now, to the Lapp Woman's hut.

REINDEER: *Oh, Lapland, sweet Lapland. . . .*

ROBBER GIRL: Ohhhh, shut your big Lapland up!

GERDA: I'll take good care of him, I promise.

ROBBER GIRL: Listen, don't let this old rug fool you, and if worse comes to worse, you can always eat him. Now hear this at last. The Lapp Woman has magic, and maybe can give you some special power. I know her. I stole some snowshoes from her once. I'll write a note to her explaining everything . . . here, from the pot, on this piece of dried codfish. And here, from the fire, the black end of this stick will do as a pen. I'll write it down. "It happens that such and such and so forth da, da, do, do, da . . . right, and etcetera . . . yours truly, and so on." All right. There. That should do it. Now run. And you, long legs, see you take care of my little girl. Look to the north, and when it gets dark you will see the Northern Lights. You must follow them to the Lapp Woman's hut, which is in Lapland.

REINDEER:

> *Oh, Lapland, sweet Lapland,*
> *We raise our antlers high,*
> *Oh, Lap, Lap, Lap, Lap, Lap, Lap—*

ROBBER GIRL: Oh, sweet shut up, you hatrack, or you'll sing her to death before she gets killed naturally. Follow the Northern Lights, and they'll lead you the way. Now, then—run!

GERDA: Good-bye, good-bye.

ROBBER GIRL: Farewell! And if you steal my reindeer, you shall dance in his place. Ha, ha, ha, ha, ha.

(The ROBBER GIRL draws her knife and pistol and begins laughing and dancing around the fire as GERDA and the REINDEER go off.)

Curtain

(And on the apron of the stage GERDA and the REINDEER dance, acting out the hardships and danger of their journey north.)

THE DANCE OF THE NORTHERN LIGHTS

Blackout

SCENE 3

AT RISE: *Days later. The LAPP WOMAN's hut. A fireplace, a pot over the flames. Poor furnishings, a table, two chairs, a bed. The REINDEER and GERDA are standing while the LAPP WOMAN reads the message on the piece of dried codfish. She may be the same woman who plays GRANDMA now dressed in ragged furs, sweaty and grimy. She looks them up and down, grunting her opinion, and reads some more. GERDA and the REINDEER are looking much the worse for wear.*

LAPP WOMAN: Um. Hmmmmm. Yes, yes, um, um, yes. So. The little brat is still alive? I'm not surprised. Hah! She could steal the sand out of an hourglass. She'll get

along. *(Takes a bite of the dried codfish.)* And so she sends you to me for help? Did she send along a pair of snowshoes? No? Well, that's like her. Asking for charity and wants it given barefoot. She'll ask to be hanged with a silk rope, that one.

GERDA: Oh, please, we were told you might help us. We've been lost, we've nearly starved. . . .

REINDEER: We've fled from bears, and fought wolves . . . and . . . and whatnot.

LAPP WOMAN: Whatnots? You've fought with whatnots . . . and still alive? Amazing! Well, you look the worse for it, that's a fact. So there you are, hungry and cold, sent along by bad luck. No one with good luck ever comes to visit. Beggars and robbers, that's my company.

REINDEER: We do beg for your help, but we are not robbers. Her name is Gerda, and she is searching for a friend. . . .

GERDA: For my friend . . . for poor Kai. The Snow Queen has stolen him away. Oh, please help us!

LAPP WOMAN: Yes, yes, yes. *(Takes another bite of the codfish.)* I have all the news. I'm chewing on it. We'll get around to that, my dear. What you need now is some hot soup. Then we'll put you in a warm bed. *(She helps GERDA to sit, then ladles up some soup in a bowl.)* There you are, darling. Eat, now, and then you'll sleep.

(*The* LAPP WOMAN *moves aside to stand by the* REIN-DEER. GERDA *says grace, then eats. After a few sips of the soup she lays her head on her arm and falls asleep. The* LAPP WOMAN *talks to the* REINDEER *aside.*)

LAPP WOMAN: See, she's almost dead already, the way you've worn her out. You should be boiled for that. Well, it's true enough. Kai has flown with the Snow Queen to her palace. He's not the first.

REINDEER: Then Kai is lost? There's no saving him? He's frozen to death?

LAPP WOMAN: Not quite yet, but he's in great danger. The cold is touching on his heart.

REINDEER: Then we must go to him. You must give us some power, some potion or spell, something to make Gerda as strong as ten men, something magic.

LAPP WOMAN: Ha, ha, ha! Ten men, yes, that ought to do it. And you want some magic? You'll be sorry for too much magic, believe me. And I can't give her any greater power than she already has. Don't you see how both man and beast must serve her? That's because she's a sweet, innocent child, and has a warm and loving heart.

GERDA: (*Talking in her troubled sleep.*) Kai, don't go. It's too dangerous. Kai, be careful. I love you.

(*The* LAPP WOMAN *takes* GERDA *from the table, sleep-walks her to the bed, and lays her gently down.*)

LAPP WOMAN: No, she'll have no need of magic, and magic has a sort of chill to it anyway. It is love and warmth that are needed now, and there are yet dangers in the way, and perhaps battles to be fought, because you know that the Imps fight on the side of the Snow Queen.

REINDEER: Then it's a battle if it must be. We'll fight the Imps or whatever else. We'll need weapons, armor. . . .

LAPP WOMAN: Hush, now, hush. She's sleeping.

(The LAPP WOMAN *begins singing a lullaby to* GERDA *and removes her boots. The* REINDEER *goes to the table. He opens a drawer and takes out knives, wooden spoons, lids of pots, utensils. He bangs a pot to test it for a helmet, bangs on a large lid to test it for a shield, clashes knives together, and begins to strap and gird himself for battle. The* LULLABY *is somewhat distressed by this racket.)*

LULLABY

Life is a fair - y tale, Sweet dreams to - night,

Life is a fairy tale,
Sweet dreams tonight,
Hansel and Gretel,
Lovely Snow White.

Life is a fairy tale,
Be of good cheer,

Dream of Prince Charming
Sleep now, my dear.

Life is a fairy tale,
Little Bo Peep,
Poor Cinderella,
Now go to sleep.

(The LAPP WOMAN tucks GERDA in, goes over to REINDEER and smacks him on his pot helmet with a big wooden spoon.)

LAPP WOMAN: Sit down, rattle brain! Here, eat. *(She fills him a bowl of soup.)*

REINDEER: We'll fight our way to Kai! We'll fight the Imps and whatever else. We'll need armor, weapons.

LAPP WOMAN: Quiet! Eat! Eat and listen! Iron and steel can only win a part of the battle. You must also fight against ice, and forgetfulness. The Snow Queen sits on her throne in the palace in the middle of a frozen lake. It is there that Kai sits at her feet, nearly frozen to death, but happy to be with her.

REINDEER: Please pass the pepper. Now how is this? Kai is freezing to death in the Snow Queen's palace, but wants to stay there? This is very good soup.

LAPP WOMAN: Glad you like it. Yes, his mind is numb from the cold. He hardly remembers who he is, or how he got there. His heart is becoming a lump of ice, the same as hers. Ice freezes to ice. Besides that, she's given him a new sled.

REINDEER: Please pass the salt. Excellent soup, I must say. Just a pinch of oregano, I think. So then, a new sled, and he is enchanted, is that it? I must have the recipe for this soup.

LAPP WOMAN: What you don't know won't

hurt you. Yes—enchanted, bewitched, in love, or whatever you want to call it.

REINDEER: Then we'll take fire to thaw him out, torches, hot coals! What kind of soup did you say this was?

LAPP WOMAN: I didn't say. Fire, torches, hot coals? No! Can't you listen? Kai's heart can only be melted by human love. Only Gerda can save him. You might call it cousin soup.

REINDEER: Cousin soup? Indeed? Well, my compliments to your cousin. But it seems that soup is all you can offer us. Hah! And we were told that you could give us magic and power. No. You leave it all up to a little girl. So there it is, hot soup is the most help you can give us. I thank you for that, but it seems like cold help where we are going.

LAPP WOMAN: Power? I have told you of Gerda's power. There is no greater power than love. And I can show you the way to the Snow Queen's palace to test that power. And you speak of soup, hot soup? Clear the table! Indeed, there is hot soup where you are going, hotter soup that ever you could care to wade through. Clear the table, clear the table! *(The* LAPP WOMAN *gets the pot from the fireplace and sets it on the table.)* I have told you something of the past. That is cold soup. And what is happening now is only simmering soup. But now you shall see a vision of the future, and the future is on the boil! Stand back! I must sweat to do this. To hang over the future is to hang over a steaming pot. Give room or you'll be scalded! Here is the hot soup you'll soon be in.

(The LAPP WOMAN *leans over the pot and begins reciting her visions, mumbling in tongues, emphasizing her excitement by banging with the spoon on the table, on the* REINDEER, *etc.* GERDA *begins moving in her sleep fitfully, tossing about and moaning.* BATTLE MUSIC *up.)*

LAPP WOMAN: There, there, now it's coming clear, and now I see it! Look, look, there it is, the boiling, bubbling future! Stand back or you'll be splashed! Now I see it—outside the Snow Queen's palace. A vision! A vision! Imps, and Devils, and Demons! There they come, one, two, many. But now, look! Look, now there are Angels—Angels coming to fight on your side. There! Look! Look, a battle! A battle! Imps and Angels! I have the vision! It's a battle! Imps and Angels! A battle, a battle!

(During this recitation, the MUSIC *has been growing, and now as* IMPS *and* ANGELS *come onstage the* BATTLE MUSIC *plays out.)*

THE BATTLE OF THE IMPS AND ANGELS

(As the IMPS *and* ANGELS *battle,* GERDA *becomes more restless, and at last thrashes about in a nightmare and cries out.)*

GERDA: Help, help, help, help, help!

(The REINDEER *joins in the battle, protecting* GERDA *as* IMPS *attempt to carry her off.)*

LAPP WOMAN: There is hot soup for you! And this is only the *dream* of a battle. Hot soup, hot soup! There's your future. Hot soup! Go jump into it!

(BATTLE MUSIC and battle up, and . . .)

$$C \quad u \quad r \quad t \quad a \quad i \quad n$$

$$\boxed{\text{S C E N E} \quad 4}$$

AT RISE: *The* SNOW QUEEN's *palace, she on her throne in the middle of a frozen lake, ice walls and a roof of ice, and ice stalactites hanging down. There are several* FROZEN BOYS *sitting about. The* SNOW QUEEN *descends and moves among them.* KAI *sits near the throne, following her motions with stiff movements of his head. His new sled sits on a pedestal next to the throne. The* SNOW QUEEN *sings.*

LOVE SONG

No sorrow, regret, and no tears,

No weeping for love that has died,

No tossing about on the tide.

Never fear, I know best,

To be empty of hope,

Don't you just love all this snow?

(The FROZEN BOYS *can yet creak their heads and crack their voices just a bit, and they respond.*)

FROZEN BOYS: NO.

SNOW QUEEN:

No sorrow, regret, and no tears,

No passion to pound at your heart,

No memory to tear you apart,

Never fear, I know best,

Flying off in my sleigh,

Wasn't it fun, would you say?

FROZEN BOYS: NAY.

SNOW QUEEN:

No sorrow, regret, and no tears,

No wondering why love has changed,

No more of that heartbreaking pain,

Never fear, I know best,

Here where the sun doesn't shine,

Isn't it great to be mine?

FROZEN BOYS: *NEIN.*

SNOW QUEEN: Naturally, my dear, dear, boys, you will have some objections at first. But you will come to know that this is the most perfect of all loves, never-changing and as cold as all eternity. You should properly thank me, for I have saved you from the great, agonizing experience of love in the warm and turnabout world. Your objections are noted, however. The nerves twitch for a while, that's all.

And you, Kai, very soon you shall love me as perfectly as all these others. I have saved a special kiss for you, Kai, and when you have that you shall have all my secrets. Now, Kai, I shall stand over here, by your new sled, for you must come to me for this kiss. Stand, Kai, and come to me, and I shall be your love forever. *(KAI in his half-frozen state rises and comes toward her.)* Come closer, Kai, into my arms. Come closer!

(KAI comes into the circle of her arms. She wraps him in an embrace and is just about to kiss him when there comes the blast of the BATTLE MUSIC, and the REINDEER and GERDA tumble in through a door of the throne room and sprawl on the floor. They are armed, and the REINDEER gets up, facing offstage in a stance for more battle.)

REINDEER: Run, Gerda, run! I'll hold them off from here. *(Goes out.)*

GERDA: *(Whirling about and seeing* KAI.*)* Kai! Kai! I've found you! Kai, we're together! I've found you.

SNOW QUEEN: *(Standing up and letting loose of* KAI, *who slumps into a frozen, sitting position.)* Who are you? Don't you dare come toward me. I am the Snow Queen. What are you doing in my palace? Guards! Guards! Chickens, guards!

GERDA: *(Brushing past the* SNOW QUEEN *and kneeling to embrace* KAI.*)* Kai, Kai. Oh, move, Kai, move a little. It's Gerda, it's Gerda, Kai!

SNOW QUEEN: Get out of here! Now, leave at once, that is an order! You are in the Snow Queen's palace. That boy is mine! Out! Out! Guards! Chickens!

GERDA: Oh, Kai, move a little, Kai, live a little longer. Oh, you're so cold, so cold.

REINDEER: *(Shouting from offstage.)* Gerda, Gerda, be ready! They're breaking through! I can't hold them off!

(The BATTLE MUSIC *comes up every time* REINDEER *shouts out from offstage, and down as the focus changes to* GERDA *and* KAI.*)*

SNOW QUEEN: Get away from him! Guards, chickens! Come to me! He's mine, don't touch him, he's mine! Guards, chickens! Come to your queen! A thief is in my palace. Guards, chickens! *(She rushes off to collect her* CHICKEN *guards.)*

GERDA: Oh, he's frozen. Oh, so cold. Oh, he's dead. Oh, Kai!

REINDEER: *(Comes onstage, shouts his lines and goes off to fight some more.)* Run, Gerda, run! Find another way out. I can't hold against them!

GERDA: No, no, I can't leave. Save yourself. Oh, Kai, don't be dead. *(Weeping and hugging* KAI.*)*

REINDEER: *(*BATTLE MUSIC *up.* REINDEER *comes onstage.)* Gerda, there are too many, I can't hold them! But look, there are Angels coming! We've got a chance, Gerda. Leave him. Run.

GERDA: Too late, too late. Run, save yourself. I can't leave. It doesn't matter. Oh, I love you, Kai, I love you. Don't be frozen, Kai, don't be dead, Kai.

REINDEER: *(*BATTLE MUSIC *up.)* Gerda . . . now! They're moving away, they're fighting the Angels. We can run! Leave him, leave him and save yourself!

(And now, as GERDA *weeps over* KAI *and kisses him, the* BOYS *begin to show movement and life.* BATTLE MUSIC *down as the* DANCE MUSIC *comes up, and the* FROZEN BOYS *begin to move, and rise up, and dance, regaining the use of their limbs.)*

THE DANCE OF THE
FROZEN BOYS

Presto

(Near the end of the dance, this dialogue as KAI comes to himself.)

GERDA: Kai, you moved! You're alive!

KAI: Gerda, oh, Gerda. I've been so cold. I couldn't move. What is this place?

GERDA: We're in the Snow Queen's palace. We're fighting a battle with the Imps. They're outside now. Angels are fighting on our side. We've got to run. Here now, stand, I'll help you.

REINDEER: *(The* DANCE *is ended, and strongly again the* BATTLE MUSIC *is up until the end of the battle.)* Quickly, Gerda! The way is clear now. We've got a chance.

GERDA: Can you stand, Kai? Can you run?

KAI: I can move, Gerda, I can move again. I'm free, I'm free!

REINDEER: Now, Gerda, now! *(He takes hold of* KAI *also.)* Run or we're lost.

(But now the outside battle forces its way through inside, and

IMPS *and* ANGELS *tumble through the door. The* FROZEN BOYS *join in, and all about is tumult as* GERDA *shouts above it.)*

G E R D A : Get up, Kai! We've got to fight our way out! Stand and fight!

K A I : I'm free, Gerda, I'm free! I can move!

R E I N D E E R : Run, now, run or we're lost!

(The SNOW QUEEN *enters with some* CHICKEN *guards, and she snaps her whip and orders them to action.)*

S N O W   Q U E E N : That one, that one! Seize him! Seize the girl! *(The* CHICKENS *run to* KAI, *but he evades them. They capture* GERDA *and pinion her as the* REINDEER *is engaged fighting a couple of* IMPS, *and the* SNOW QUEEN *calls out more orders.)* Kill her, kill her! Kill the boy! Kill them all!

G E R D A : Kai, help me, help me, Kai! Help! Help!

*(KAI *must act alone. He breaks off an ice stalactite for a sword and wades into the* CHICKENS, *whaling away, yelling his war whoop.)*

K A I : I'll save you, Gerda. Blam, blam, blam, blam! It's that daredevil Kai with his new sled he got for Christmas! Blam, blam, blam, blam!

(The FROZEN BOYS *and the* ANGELS *are winning, and they force the* IMPS *out the door, shouting and whacking away.*

KAI *and the* REINDEER *rout the* CHICKENS *and* GERDA, *freed from the hold of a* CHICKEN, *jumps on the* SNOW QUEEN's *back and they tussle on the floor. For a few minutes, the melee continues, till at last all disentangle. The* SNOW QUEEN *and* CHICKENS *retreat offstage. Left alone onstage, the* BATTLE MUSIC *fading to silence, are* GERDA, KAI, *and* REINDEER.)

GERDA: Oh, Kai! My hero! You rescued me, Kai, you saved me!

KAI: Let me at 'em, it's Kai to the rescue! Blam, blam, blam, blam! Down he dives off of Kill-Devil Hill, blam, blam, blam!

REINDEER: *(Restraining him.)* No, no, they've gone, we've won. The way is clear now. We've got to run! *(To* GERDA.*)* I think he's a little delirious, the sudden heat and all.

KAI: Yes, yes, back to Grandma's before the cookies are burned. But first of all I'll just pick up my new sled.

(But now the SNOW QUEEN *re-enters with more* CHICKENS, *all clucking for a fight!)*

GERDA: Here they come again! There are more of them! Run, run!

KAI: Let me at 'em! Blam, blam, blam . . .

*(*BATTLE MUSIC *up briefly. But the* REINDEER *and*

GERDA *drag* KAI *to the door, and all go out, and the music fades with a dying strain as the* SNOW QUEEN *is left alone onstage with her* CHICKENS.)

SNOW QUEEN: Leave me alone. Go, all of you. Go back to the sleigh. I'll be along presently. *(Off the* CHICKENS *go. The* SNOW QUEEN *stands alone, forlorn.)* Run off, then, run off to the melting world! Desert me, then! Betray me! Your love was not perfect, and I shall not weep for you. Go! Find a love like mine if you can. There is nothing but pain and heartbreak out there. You'll be back, happy to freeze again. But I shall remain like I am, never to change. Alone . . . cold . . . eternal . . . perfect, as all things that do not change are perfect. I am the Snow Queen. And I shall never regret, nor remember, and I shall never cry. Never . . . never . . . never.

Curtain

SCENE 5

LIGHTS UP: *On the apron of the stage, the* CHIEF IMP *and the* "INVENTOR" IMP.

CHIEF: What!? Is that it? You let the Snow Queen lose? Is that the end? You mean our Imps were beaten by those . . . those . . . !

IMP: Angels, Your Highness.

CHIEF: Those "religious flying objects"!! You will be shot at dawn — *after* the alligators.

IMP: It was only a setback, Your Highness. At this very moment the scene is changing.

CHIEF: She was about to cry.

IMP: It would be difficult to tell, Your Highness. We'll watch some more. But right now the Sparrows are going to dance.

CHIEF: The Sparrows have already danced.

IMP: Those were Spring Sparrows, Your Highness. These are Snow Sparrows. And after all, what can one do about Sparrows?

CHIEF: That's true. All right, let 'em dance. *(IMPS leave the apron as the* SPARROWS *come on.)*

DANCE OF THE SPARROWS
(Reprise)

Blackout

AT RISE: *Christmas Day,* GRANDMA*'s parlor. Same setting as before, but now with a Christmas tree and holiday hangings.* KAI *and* GERDA *are among the crowd of* CHILDREN, *all freely dipping their mugs into a large punch bowl on the central table, and stuffing on cookies from a large platter. They bustle about to a reprise of the music of the . . .*

CHILDREN'S DANCE
(R e p r i s e)

1ST CHILD: And lift your glasses high for a toast to Kai, for telling the biggest lie of the winter.

KAI: It wasn't a lie!

2ND CHILD: Then it was a dream. Flying in the sky with the Snow Queen, and a battle with Imps and Angels at the North Pole.

3RD CHILD: Oh, the Snow Queen who glitters like ice and carries a white fox muff and silver whip.

GERDA: It's true, it's all true. I saw her myself. It isn't a lie, and it wasn't a dream.

CHILDREN: Oh, we should believe Gerda, she talks with flowers. And French-speaking blackbirds, *parlez-vous.* And a singing reindeer from Lapland.

(The CHILDREN *stand at attention, saluting, and sing.)*

Oh, Lapland, sweet Lapland,
We raise our antlers high. . . .

KAI: It's true, it's true, everything Gerda said.

1ST CHILD: Someone who says he has flown through the air behind six white chickens would believe anything.

2ND CHILD: They were bewitched by the Lapp Woman, that's what happened.

GERDA: She wasn't a witch. She was kind, and she helped us, and saved us from starving. . . .

GRANDMA: *(Entering with another platter of cookies.)* Here, here, here! Let us have some peace and quiet for just a few minutes. Children, children! For a minute, please. Quiet, quiet! Thank you. How delighted I am to have you all here on Christmas Day. And how happy I'm sure we all are to have Kai and Gerda safely back with us.

And now for a moment let us bow our heads and behave ourselves. And we will give thanks for the many gifts of our lives and for all our blessings. Please bow your heads. Let us remember, O Lord, those little ones who are not so favored as we are, who are without comfort and protection, who are without home and family and must suffer hunger and the cruelty of neglect. And on this most holy and silent night . . .

(BANG, BANG, BANG, *thumping at the door.* GRANDMA *holds up a hand that they will finish the prayer.)*

. . . this most holy and silent night . . . *(BANG, BANG, BANG!)* . . . holy and silent . . . *(BANG, BANG!)* . . . and furthermore . . . amen.

R O B B E R   G I R L : Hallo, hallo! Is everybody dead in there? Anybody home? Open the door or I'll shoot the lock off. Stand still, you horned toad, or I'll have your kidneys on toast. *(BANG, BANG!)* Open, I say!

G R A N D M A :   Good heavens, whoever is that?

G E R D A :   A friend, a friend!

(GERDA *flings open the door, and in comes the* ROBBER GIRL *with a swirl of snow, her pistol and dagger stuck in her belt The* REINDEER *sticks his head inside.)*

R O B B E R   G I R L : Sorry for all the racket, but we haven't got all day to stand on doorsteps. It's a business trip You'll excuse us.

G R A N D M A : Oh, be careful, stand back, she has a pistol!

G E R D A : *(Throws her arms around the* ROBBER GIRL.*)* Oh, I'm so happy to see you! Oh, this is the very best Christmas! And you, oh my brave Lapland! *(To the* CHILDREN.*)* This is my dear friend that I've told you about. She saved our lives, and this native of Lapland and myself, we fought bears, and Imps, and wolves together.

REINDEER: And . . . ah . . . whatnot.

(Subdued greeting from the CHILDREN.*)*

ROBBER GIRL: Hello yourself. Can the beast step inside?

GERDA: Oh, please. Oh, Lapland, how happy I am to see you. *(Hugs and kisses* REINDEER.*)* Can you stay and sing with us?

REINDEER: Sing? I love to sing. *(*SINGS, *saluting.)*

    Oh, Lapland, sweet Lapland . . .

ROBBER GIRL: Ohhhhhhh, give us a Christmas holiday on that!

(But the CHILDREN *are delighted at this, and push and chatter among themselves to get close to the* REINDEER.*)*

CHILDREN: Oh, he does sing! He's real, feel his fur. It's magic. Isn't he wonderful! Then it all did happen. It was true, it was all true.

ROBBER GIRL: Oh, leave him alone, leave him alone. Next thing he'll want is Christmas cards. No time for singing and all that nonsense, we've got to be on our way.

GERDA: Oh, please stay, dear friends, please stay.

ROBBER GIRL: No blubbering, no blubbering! What a time of year for blubbering. Easy come, easy go, that's the way to look at the world. And which one is Kai, causing all this trouble in the first place?

KAI: That's me, I'm Kai.

ROBBER GIRL: Hmpt! Well, I wonder if it was worth all the trouble. *(To GERDA.)* I'm alone now, you see, except for this excuse of a Reindeer. *(She draws her pistol and begins waving it about, at which GRANDMA cries out and shrinks away in fright.)* But, oh, the fun we've had you wouldn't believe, the robbing we've done, the hangings we've escaped! But no time for that. Listen, now, I have some news. First of all from the flowers. They greet you.

GERDA: Oh, the beautiful flowers. Are they still so in love and so sad?

ROBBER GIRL: It's all very tiresome. And then Sweetheart said bon jar, or something.

GERDA: Did the Crow learn his lessons? Does he live in the castle with Sweetheart now?

ROBBER GIRL: For a while he did. Then he ran off with a French Hen. It's all a lot of nonsense. Let's see, something else. Oh, I was traveling north, and the Lapp Woman says hello. And one more thing, what was it? Oh, yes, there's presents for you. Bend your back down, mop tail! Now what's in this pack? It's for Kai. Never did like fancy wrappings. It looks like a sled.

KAI: Oh, it's my sled! My new sled!

ROBBER GIRL: That's right. It's the intention that counts, not that I care. Break a leg. And what else? Oh, this is for Gerda.

GERDA: Ohhhhh, a white fox muff!

ROBBER GIRL: That's all, don't bother thanking me. Off we go. We can't stay in one place too long. Not good for our necks, you understand.

GERDA: But it's a party, and we're going to sing.

ROBBER GIRL: Singing is all very well if you've got nothing better to do. But it's a good day for robbing. Everyone is stuffed with goose and pudding, worn out from all the kissing and hugging, and their brains are full of cranberries. You can snatch their silver and get thanked for it. More blessed to give than to receive, you know. So there's business to be about, and off we go. Out the door, beast. Out, out! Before you forget your manners. Farewell, farewell.

REINDEER: Good-bye, good-bye, Gerda; good-bye, Kai; good-bye, children.

GERDA: Good-bye, good-bye.

CHILDREN: Good-bye, good-bye.

(ROBBER GIRL and REINDEER exit.)

GRANDMA: Glory be to God! Thank heavens they're gone! Good gracious, oh, sweet angels, I thought she was going to shoot off that pistol!

ROBBER GIRL: *(Banging the door open.)* Oh, I almost forgot. *(She leaps onto the table and raises her pistol high.)* Merry Christmas! *(Fires the pistol. BLAM! Jumps down, runs out and slams door and is gone.)*

GRANDMA: Ohhhhhhhh . . . ohhhhh. . . . .

(GRANDMA *faints onto a sofa, and someone fans her face. She recovers during the* FINALE, *and* ALL *the* PLAYERS *come out a few at a time until* ALL *are onstage and singing at the end of the* FINALE.)

FINALE

Deep is the winter, dark and long,
Dark is the day that has no song,
Come near the fire, sing in praise,
This is the season's brightest day.

Deep is the snow that never melts,
Cold is the heart that hides itself,
Come near the fire, sing in praise,
This is the season's warmest day.

The tree is trimmed, the fire is lit,
To wish you Merry Christmas.
Good friends are close, the clocks all tick,
To wish you Merry Christmas.
Beneath the mistletoe we kiss,
To wish you Merry Christmas.
Our love for you goes with our gift,
To wish you Merry Christmas.

Deep is the winter, dark and long,
Dark is the day that has no song.
Come near the fire, sing in praise,
This is the season's warmest, brightest day.

Deep is the win-ter dark and long, Dark is the day that

has no song, Come near the fi-re, sing in praise,

This is the sea-son's bright-est day.

Deep is the snow that nev-er melts, Cold is the heart that

hides it-self, Come near the fi-re, sing in praise,

This is the sea-son's warm-est day. Double time The

tree is trimmed, the fire is lit, To wish you Mer-ry Christ-mas. Good friends are close, the clocks all tick, To

Final Curtain

The Snow Queen
A Christmas Pageant
Text & lyrics copyright © 1996 by Richard Kennedy
Illustrations copyright © 1996 by Edward S. Gazsi
Music copyright © 1996 by Mark Lambert

Library of Congress Cataloging-in-Publication Data
Kennedy, Richard, date
    The snow queen : a Christmas pageant / adapted by Richard Kennedy ; music by Mark
Lambert ; pictures by Edward S. Gazsi.
        p.   cm.
    "A Laura Geringer book."
    Summary: A little girl enlists the help of a robber and a reindeer to save her best friend from
an evil Snow Queen who steals little boys and freezes them.
    ISBN 0-06-027115-9. — ISBN 0-06-027116-7 (lib. bdg.)
    1. Children's plays, American.   2. Fairy tales—Adaptations.   [1. Plays.   2. Fairy Tales—
Adaptations.]   I. Gazsi, Edward S., ill.   II. Andersen, H. C. (Hans Christian), 1805–1875.
Snedronningen.   III. Title.
PS3561.E42713H36   1996   95-52211
812'.54—dc20   CIP
                                                                                      AC

Typography by Christine Kettner
1   2   3   4   5   6   7   8   9   10
❖
First Edition